little books for

BUSY MOMS

Great Books
to Read and
Fun Things
to Do With Them

Resources from MOPS

Books

Beyond Macaroni and Cheese
A Cure for the Growly Bugs and Other Tips for Moms
Getting Out of Your Kids' Faces and Into Their Hearts
Little Books for Busy Moms
    Time Out for Mom ... Ahhh Moments
    Great Books to Read and Fun Things to Do with Them
    If You Ever Needed Friends, It's Now
    Kids' Stuff and What to Do with It
Loving and Letting Go
Mom to Mom
Meditations for Mothers
A Mother's Footprints of Faith
Ready for Kindergarten
What Every Child Needs
What Every Mom Needs
When Husband and Wife Become Mom and Dad

Books with Drs. Henry Cloud and John Townsend

Raising Great Kids
Raising Great Kids for Parents of Preschoolers Workbook
Raising Great Kids for Parents of Teenagers Workbook
Raising Great Kids for Parents of School-Age Children Workbook

Gift Books

God's Words of Life from the Mom's Devotional Bible
Mommy, I Love You Just Because

Kids Books

Little Jesus, Little Me
My Busy, Busy Day
See the Country, See the City
Mommy, May I Hug the Fishes?
Mad Maddie Maxwell
Zachary's Zoo
Morning, Mr. Ted
Boxes, Boxes Everywhere
Snug as a Bug?

Bible

Mom's Devotional Bible

Audio

Raising Great Kids

Curriculum

Raising Great Kids for Parents of Preschoolers *Zondervan*Groupware™
(with Drs. Henry Cloud and John Townsend)

little books for

BUSY MOMS

Great Books to Read and Fun Things to Do with Them

MOTHERS OF
M♥PS.
PRESCHOOLERS

MARY BETH LAGERBORG general editor
written by JANE C. JARRELL

ZondervanPublishingHouse
Grand Rapids, Michigan

A Division of HarperCollinsPublishers

Great Books to Read and Fun Things to Do with Them
Copyright © 2000 by Jane C. Jarrell

Requests for information should be addressed to:

ZondervanPublishingHouse
Grand Rapids, Michigan 49530

Library of Congress Cataloging-in-Publication Data

Jarrell, Jane Cabaniss, 1961-
    Great books to read and fun things to do with them /
Mary Beth Lagerborg, general editor ; written by Jane C. Jarrell.
      p.   cm.
    ISBN 0-310-23515-4 (softcover)
    1. Best books--Children's literature. 2. Children's literature--
Bibliography. 3.Children--Books and reading--Activity pro-
grams. I. Lagerborg, Mary Beth. II. Title. III. Series.
Z1037.J37   2000
[PN1009.A1]
028'.8'083--dc21   00-043280
                                        CIP

Published in association with the literary agency of Alive
Communications, Inc., 7680 Goddard Street, Suite 200, Colorado
Springs, CO 80920.

Interior design by Melissa Elenbaas

Interior Illustrations by Thomas Ungrey

Printed in the United States of America

00 01 02 03 04 05 / ❖ DC/ 10 9 8 7 6 5 4 3 2 1

For
Sarah Allegra
and
Chelsey Elizabeth
May we have many days
with great books,
fun foods, and creative designs.
You are both so special!

Contents

Help for Busy Moms

I LIKE TO STUDY moms in the grocery checkout line, moms with a child in the cart grabbing at the tantalizing gum and candy displays. Usually these moms don't resemble the women posed on the magazine covers next to them. These women are on a mission: to feed and care for their families while at the same time teaching their children to make good food choices, to not pull things off the shelves, to not whine, and to stay close to the cart. No matter what their size or shape or age or education or experience, they're trying to be the best moms they can be.

To be the best they can be, moms solicit advice from parenting experts and mothers and grandmothers. But sometimes the best help of all comes from other moms who, traveling the same road, have made some great discoveries they're willing to pass along. Thus the series Little Books for Busy Moms was born. We've chosen topics to meet the needs of moms, presented in a format they can read quickly and easily.

One thing moms need is simple ideas to make the most of those wonderful "teachable moments" with their children. Author Jane Jarrell works as a food stylist for print and film in addition to writing books and magazine articles. She has organized and directed cooking shows for *Southern Living* magazine and was food editor for Neiman Marcus's *Pigtails and Froglegs* cookbook. Now her daughter, Sarah, age four, is her kitchen companion and favorite food tester and taster. Jane enjoys using her expertise with foods and crafts to stretch the joy of snuggle-and-read times with her daughter.

Here is a treat just for you, Mom. You can enjoy it in little bits and pieces or all at once. We hope that, in little ways or large, what you find here will make a lasting difference.

MARY BETH LAGERBORG
PUBLISHING MANAGER,
MOPS INTERNATIONAL (MOTHERS OF
PRESCHOOLERS)

Personally Speaking

MOTHERHOOD HAS ROCKED MY world. Never in my wildest dreams could I have prepared myself for such an all-important, all-consuming responsibility. Each day has brought new opportunities for me to learn as well as teach. Each day uncharted waters ripple with excitement as to what my daughter will do, what she will say, and which relative she will resemble. Thus far, my four years of mommyhood have left me feeling inadequate some days, joyful other days, sleepless some nights, and cuddled with a little miracle other nights.

Watching my child explore her new world has been the most fascinating part of the day-to-day privilege of being a mom. From the first time she sat up, to walking, then talking, each new experience has offered a time for my daughter to learn.

Like many children, one of my daughter's favorite pastimes is listening to me read her books, perhaps because reading opens the door to all things imaginable. As I have read, snuggled, explained, and read again and again the same stories, I have watched her mind absorb everything on the colorful pages. Questions and ideas, thoughts and values have started to mold her heart and mind as she enjoys our reading time together.

I too have fallen in love with the wonderfully creative stories we read together, and it quickly became natural for me to want to expand our beloved stories into more, using activities involving art and foods.

Ultimately, a book was born. By taking great books that had a solid story line as the base and expanding their morals into fun activities, I knew I had hit upon an idea that could be a terrific teaching tool. Believing we have one shot at motherhood, I want to maximize every opportunity to guide my child to understand right from wrong. Our choices as mothers today become *their* choices tomorrow. My fervent desire is that my choices today will ensure that my daughter's choices tomorrow will be grounded in God's truths and moral precepts.

Our daughter was born when I was a little older—not in my twenties. Prior to her arrival, I had always worked full-time outside the home. My first work experience was with *Southern Living* magazine, where I began to learn all about food, from recipe development to the final presentation. It was the presentation that began my interest in combining art with food. The beautiful pictures you see in food magazines are prepared by hands that painstakingly tend to the details until all is ready for the camera.

Food preparation for the camera became my next occupation. As a food stylist, I prepared food for television, print magazines, and newspaper food sections. My love of working with food has made my special times with my daughter extra fun; we cook and create with a whole new zest. She has given me an entirely different set of eyes to envision what a child sees as she begins to explore the world of food.

I hope you too will see the fabulous opportunities awaiting you and your child as you read the stories suggested and create your own special times with art and food.

How to Use This Book

READING OPENS THE WORLD to a child. But now that her world is open and you have her interest piqued, how do you take the experience to the next level? Have you ever wished for something else to work with to further emphasize the lessons being taught within the pages?

Great Books to Read and Fun Things to Do with Them provides a beautiful complementary package by tying together favorite children's stories with activities to reinforce the story being read. This book offers cooking, art, and moral precepts as layers to build with after reading the suggested book. And it does not stop there; it continues with a verse from the Bible, which secures the learning package like a large and beautiful bow.

ACTIVITY-BASED LEARNING

Let's face it—parenting is hard. Add the responsibility of instilling lifelong values and principles that we as parents want to pass on, and you've gone from hectic to one huge guilt trip. Exactly when between soccer, birthday parties, ballet, and school is there time to teach our children all the priceless principles they need to hold in life?

Great Books to Read and Fun Things to Do with Them is designed to help solve this problem by providing children and parents natural teaching and learning time through two activities children love: cooking and art. Teachers have known for years that these multisensory practices are wonderful ways to teach. We have chosen an assortment of children's favorite books and have extended their life lessons into fun yet practical projects for parents and children to share.

HAVE A PLAN

To make the most of the recipes and art activities in this book, try the following helpful suggestions:

1. Check out the book of the month from the library or purchase it from your favorite bookstore.

2. Decide which activity you would like to use to extend the principles in the selected story.

3. Read the recipe or art project to determine how many children are appropriate for the particular activity. If you are working in a group of more than four or five, definitely consider asking another parent to help.

4. Pick a time of the week that is least busy and stressful for everyone. Determine to have a relaxing, fun time.

5. Review the art projects and recipes to make sure you have the appropriate materials and that you have allotted enough preparation time. Some steps may need to be done the day before in order to finish the recipes in the length of time you have (for instance, cookie dough that needs to be refrigerated for several hours).

DON'T FORGET TO PREPARE

- Each activity will have a "Things You'll Need" box and an ingredient or supplies section as easy references for setting up cooking and art trays ahead of time. Allow the children to pour, measure, and glue, but have all of these ingredients ready in advance.

- Any preparation that needs to be done by you, such as browning meat or chopping fruit, should be done ahead of time.

- Prepare a safe cooking and working environment for the children. Seated around a large table works great, but seated on a stool next to the stove is dangerous! Many schools use individual heating units in their cooking activities, and you may find that one would be well worth the investment. For best results, plug the cord in on the side of the table where you are sitting, and have the children work opposite you.
- Discuss the safety rules before you begin, while you still have the children's full attention.

REMEMBER YOUR PURPOSE

Reading to your children is vital to opening their eyes to the fabulous world God created. Each story suggested in this book gives you a place to start and a foundation from which to build your creative time together.

Always remember ...

> I helped a little child to see
> That God had made the willow tree
> and He became more real to me.
> I tried to lead a child thru play
> To grow more Christ-like day by day
> And I myself became that way.
> I led a little child in prayer

And as we bowed in worship there
I felt anew God's loving care.
Lord, help us ever quick to see
By guiding children, we find thee.

—AUTHOR UNKNOWN

Winter Wonderful

I am always with you, to the very end.
Matthew 28:20

READ ...

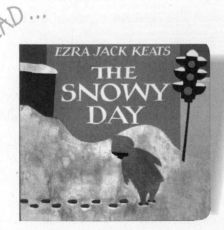

By: Ezra Jack Keats
Published by: Viking Press

THE SNOWY DAY TELLS of the quiet adventures of a young boy as he plays in the deep, deep snow. Snow clouds hang low and threatening; a winter day is surely here. January is smack dab in the middle of winter. If you live in a cold climate, scarves, mittens, and gloves are usually the requirement of the day. Think back to "snow days" when you were young, those days when school was closed because of heavy snow. Snowflakes, snowballs, and rosy cheeks made the day fly by in tantalizing style. Sledding into the frozen pond wore you out so much that you were too tired to lift your hot chocolate. When the sounds of a crackling fire are what you long to hear, nestle into your kitchen and recreate a little of the outside with these ideas.

TEACHING TIPS

The beauty of freshly fallen snow offers hours of frozen fun. When the boundless possibilities of a new snow come your way, try this idea for extra family fun: Create a snow family. Make a snowman and a snow lady to represent Mom and Dad, then create snow brothers and sisters.

Discuss with your children how God created each individual snowflake to be different, unique and special. Tell them how, in the same way, God also created each person in your family with unique and special qualities. Use this opportunity to discuss good things about each family member.

RECIPES

Tortilla Snowflakes

Things You'll Need:
wax paper
child safety scissors
2 small bowls
pastry brush
cutting board
cookie sheet
Ingredients:
8 (10-inch) flour tortillas
1/2 cup butter, melted
1/2 cup sugar
2 teaspoons cinnamon

Directions:
1. Preheat the oven to 350 degrees.
2. Place tortilla on wax-paper-covered cutting board. Fold a tortilla in half sideways and then fold in half again (similar to folding paper to cut out snowflakes). Using safety scissors, cut out small holes.
3. Unfold the tortilla and you have a snowflake; repeat with remaining tortillas.
4. Combine sugar and cinnamon in a small bowl.
5. Paint the melted butter over the tortilla snowflake with a pastry brush. Sprinkle with sugar and cinnamon.

6. Place on a cookie sheet and bake for 6 to 8 minutes.

Snow Crunch

Things You'll Need:
measuring cups
large bowl
large wooden spoon
medium microwave-safe bowl
wax paper
Ingredients:
1 cup small salty pretzels
1 cup peanuts
1 cup marshmallows
1 cup cheese crackers
1 cup raisins
1 cup small pieces chocolate candy
1 cup dried cereal
3 cups white almond bark, melted

Directions:

1. Measure all ingredients except the white almond bark into a large bowl. Stir to thoroughly combine.
2. In a medium microwave-safe bowl, melt the white almond bark in the microwave according to package directions.
3. Stir the melted white almond bark into the large bowl of ingredients until thoroughly coated.

4. Pour out onto a surface that has been covered with wax paper. Let harden.
5. When hard, break into pieces and serve.

Cherry Snowballs

Things You'll Need:
food processor or large plastic bag with
   rolling pin
large bowl
wooden spoon
measuring cup
teaspoon
airtight container
Ingredients:
1 box vanilla wafers
1 (6-ounce) can frozen cherry juice, thawed
2 cups powdered sugar
1/2 cup margarine, melted and cooled
1 cup shredded coconut

Directions:
1. Crush the wafers in a food processor, or put into a large plastic bag and roll with a rolling pin until finely crushed.
2. In a large bowl, combine crushed wafers, cherry juice, powdered sugar, and melted margarine. Stir thoroughly.
3. Let dough stand for about 30 minutes.
4. Scoop out dough with a teaspoon and roll into balls.

5. Roll the balls in shredded coconut until covered.
6. Store in an airtight container until ready to serve.

Snow Cloud Cakes

Things You'll Need:
wax paper
medium microwave-safe bowl
small bowl
wooden spoon
Ingredients:
1 large prepared angel food cake
1 package vanilla baking chips
1 container decorative silver balls (because every cloud has a silver lining)

Directions:

1. Tear large pieces from the angel food cake to form "clouds."
2. Place vanilla chips in a microwavable bowl and melt on medium in 40-second intervals. Stir until smooth.
3. Dip one side of each piece of angel food cake into the melted vanilla chips.
4. Place silver balls into a small bowl. Dip the vanilla-coated side of each "cloud" into the silver balls and place onto wax paper to harden.

ART ADVENTURES

Snowman Scene

Things You'll Need:
blue construction paper
small round white stickers
white construction paper (cut into 3 graduated
   circles)
black construction paper (for the hat, and 2
   small circles for eyes)
red construction paper (cut into triangles for
   the mouth and buttons)
orange construction paper (for the nose and
   scarf)
white glue

Directions:

1. After all the different shapes have been cut
    out, glue them onto the blue paper to form a
    snowman and landscape as simple or as elab-
    orate as desired.
2. Place round white stickers around the picture
    to resemble falling snow.

Snowy Day Shovels

Things You'll Need:
black construction paper
red construction paper
aluminum foil

11 x 14 sheet of construction paper (for
    background)
child safety scissors
Scotch tape
marker

Directions:

1. Cut a 1 1/2 inch by 8-inch strip of red con-
    struction paper for the handle.
2. Cut a 2-inch by 2-inch strip of black con-
    struction paper to connect the handle to the
    shovel.
3. Cut a 4-inch by 4-inch square of aluminum
    foil for the shovel.
4. Tape one edge of the black construction paper
    to the back of the long red strip of construc-
    tion paper. Then tape the other end of the
    black construction paper to the back of the
    aluminum foil square.
5. Glue the entire shovel to a large piece of con-
    struction paper and write underneath: "I'll
    help you shovel snow, Dad."

Toothbrush Snow Pictures

Things You'll Need:
black or dark blue construction paper
white tempera paint
paint smocks
tracing paper

old toothbrushes
pen or pencil
child safety scissors
newspaper or brown craft paper

Directions:

1. Using tracing paper, trace the outline of a
    snowman onto newspaper or brown craft
    paper; cut out.
2. Lay the snowman stencil on top of black or
    dark blue piece of construction paper.
3. Dip the toothbrush into white paint. Tap the
    brush on the edge of the paint jar to get rid of
    any extra paint that might drip onto the paper.
    Holding the brush over the paper with one
    hand, run the "pointer" finger of your other
    hand through the bristles, splattering paint
    over the entire area not covered by the snow-
    man stencil.
4. Let the paint dry before picking the snowman
    stencil off the construction paper.

Lifelong Love

Friends love at all times.
Proverbs 17:17

READ ...

By: Sam McBratney
Published by: Candlewick Press

THE LOVE BETWEEN A parent and a child is a powerful thing. This charming story depicts a conversation with Big Nutbrown Hare and Little Nutbrown Hare as they find creative ways to express how much they love each other. As far as arms can stretch, as far as upside down toes can reach, as far as they can hop. The only problem for Little Nutbrown Hare is that Big Nutbrown Hare can stretch, reach, and hop much further than he. Still, that does not stop Little Nutbrown Hare from loving Big Nutbrown Hare all the way to the moon. Read and see how Big Nutbrown Hare tops that.

TEACHING TIPS

Just as Little Nutbrown Hare and Big Nutbrown Hare explained the vastness of their love for each other, you too can take this opportunity to teach your children how to express love to others.

Involve everyone in your family as you choose a family symbol for love, like the shape of a heart. Explain to family members that whenever this symbol is found, it serves to remind them that they are special and loved. Using heart stickers or stamps, hide your family love symbol in places like the toe of your child's footy pajamas, a preschool lunch box, or on a nap time pillow. Everyone will enjoy receiving an unexpected special love surprise.

RECIPES

Hugs and Kisses

Things You'll Need:
large bowl
jelly roll pan
wax paper
table knife
heart-shaped cookie cutter
cooking spray
measuring cups
heart-shaped box
valentine tissue paper
ribbon

Ingredients:
1 box white cake mix
red food coloring
white prepared frosting
red cinnamon candies
1 bag Hershey's kisses
optional: prepared pound cake, tube icings,
    heart-shaped sprinkles

Directions:

1. Preheat oven to 350 degrees.
2. Prepare cake mix according to package directions.
3. Divide cake batter in half; add red food coloring to one bowl of batter until you get the shade of red you prefer.

4. Line jelly roll pan with wax paper. Spoon the two colors of batter into the pan in a checkerboard pattern. Swirl batters together with a table knife.

6. Bake for 15 to 20 minutes, or until a wooden toothpick comes out clean. Remove from oven and cool.

7. Cut the cooled cake with a heart-shaped cookie cutter.

8. Line a heart-shaped box with valentine tissue paper and place the heart-shaped cakes inside. Toss in some Hershey's kisses. Tie with a big red bow.

9. Optional: To do this without baking, slice a prepared frozen pound cake into about 1-inch thick slices, then cut the cake slices with heart-shaped cookie cutters. Decorate with tube icings and heart-shaped sprinkles. This makes a great teacher or neighbor gift.

"You're a Great Catch" Nibbles

Things You'll Need:
2 microwave-safe bowls
measuring spoons
wax paper
child safety scissors
netting
ribbon
construction paper
marker
hole punch

measuring cups

Ingredients:
1 bag pretzel-flavored fish crackers
2 cups vanilla baking chips
2 tablespoons heavy cream
red food coloring

Directions:
1. Divide pretzel-flavored fish crackers into two equal portions.
2. Divide vanilla baking chips into two microwave-safe bowls. Add 1 tablespoon cream to each bowl. Microwave in 30-second intervals, stirring thoroughly at each interval. Repeat until melted.
3. Add red food coloring to one bowl; in the other bowl add a little coloring for pink or leave plain for white.
4. Dip one half of each fish into one color melted white chocolate and the other half in the other color. Lay out on wax paper to dry completely.
5. Cut 8-inch squares of netting and lay them flat, filling each with 1/2 cup dipped fish. On a piece of construction paper write, "You're a great catch." Cut out a heart shape around the words, punch a hole in the top, and thread it through a ribbon.
6. Pull ends of netting toward the middle and tie with a ribbon.

Bed of Leaves Silly Salad

Things You'll Need:
knife (parent only)
paper plates
cutting board
miniature cookie cutters
Ingredients:
1 head red cabbage
1 small head iceberg lettuce
1 yellow squash
1 carrot
1 red bell pepper
1 stalk celery
1/2 cup smoked turkey, shredded
2 pieces American cheese
commercial salad dressing

Directions:

1. Gently remove red cabbage leaves from the head of cabbage, using the outside leaves to form the salad bed. Place on a paper plate.
2. Wash, dry, and tear lettuce into pieces; place in cabbage bed.
3. Create a rabbit from various vegetable pieces: cut the neck of the yellow squash into small rounds to use for eyes; cut the carrot into disks and use small cookie cutter to form the nose shape; cut and seed the red bell pepper to form the smile; slice celery into small pieces for eyebrows; place the shredded turkey all around for the fur; cut rabbit ears from American cheese and place at the top of the salad.
4. Makes two silly salads.

Marshmallow Moons

Things You'll Need:
plastic knife
paper plate
Ingredients:
rice cake
marshmallow cream
optional: chocolate syrup

Directions:

1. Place a rice cake on a paper plate.
2. Using a small plastic knife, spread a layer of marshmallow cream over the rice cake to make the moon.
3. Optional: drizzle with chocolate syrup to form clouds passing over the moon.

ART ADVENTURES

Nutbrown the Nutshell Rabbit

Things You'll Need:
child safety scissors
walnut shell half
wax paper
hole punch
black felt
pink felt
toothpick
white glue
brown yarn

Directions:

1. Place a walnut shell half on wax paper.
2. Using the hole punch, cut circles out of black felt for eyes.
3. Cut ears from the pink felt.
4. Using a toothpick, place a dot of glue onto the walnut shell and stick the felt eyes to the glue.
5. Glue the pink ears to the top of the walnut shell.
6. Cut a piece of yarn about 1 inch long and unravel it into individual strands. Cut each strand in half. Glue two strands on each side of the face to form whiskers.

Tickly Toes

Things You'll Need:
pink construction paper
blue construction paper
green construction paper
brown construction paper
child safety scissors
black marker
white yarn

Directions:

1. Have child place his or her feet on the pink construction paper. Trace around feet with a black marker.

2. Cut the feet outline and glue them to the blue construction paper, to form the rabbit's ears.
3. Cut a circle from the brown construction paper to form a face. Glue the face onto the blue construction paper just under the ears. Draw in the rabbit's eyes, nose, and mouth.
4. Cut four 2-inch pieces of yarn and fray them. Glue two pieces to each side of the nose for the whiskers.
5. Tear a 1/4-inch strip all the way across one side of the green construction paper; glue to the bottom of the blue paper to form grass.

Bed of Leaves

Things You'll Need:
newspaper
white glue
several assorted leaves
small cookie sheet
aluminum foil
paint smocks
various colors of tempera paint
shirt cardboard or poster board
small paint roller
thin white paper

Directions:

1. Prepare the work surface by covering it with newspaper. Cover the small cookie sheet with

aluminum foil. Pour a small amount of paint onto the covered cookie sheet.

2. Glue the leaves to the cardboard or poster board and set aside to dry.

3. When leaves are dry, move paint roller back and forth through the paint; then roll over the leaves.

4. Lay the thin white paper on top of the painted leaves. Gently rub your hands back and forth over the paper. Lift to see Nutbrown Hare's bed of leaves.

Making the World More Beautiful

Look at the beauty of the LORD.
Psalm 27:4

READ...

By: Barbara Cooney
Published by: Viking Press

IN *MISS RUMPHIUS* WE meet Alice Rumphius, a little girl whose grandfather had traveled to America many years ago on a very large sailing ship. Alice's grandfather would tell her wonderful stories about far away places and exciting adventures. Alice wanted to travel the world when she grew up, and after her travels, she wanted to find a lovely home by the sea—just as her grandfather had done. Her grandfather always told her one thing she must do was to think of something to make the world a more beautiful place. When Alice grew up, she did just as her grandfather had suggested, garnering her the title of the Lupine Lady.

TEACHING TIPS

Miss Rumphius wanted to travel the world and then come home to live by the sea, which she did. However, there was one very important thing her grandfather told her she must do: "Think of something to make the world more beautiful."

What can you do to make the world more beautiful? Sit down as a family and choose a once-a-month project that would help your neighborhood, school, church, or park become "more beautiful." Discuss simple ways to make the world more beautiful by sharing God's love with others, such as visiting a sick person or making some cookies for a friend.

RECIPES

Rose Soup (Alice's Porridge)

Things You'll Need:
measuring spoons
measuring cups
blender
medium bowl
Ingredients:
2 cups strawberries
1 tablespoon lemon juice
1/2 teaspoon vanilla extract
3 ounces cream cheese

Directions:
1. Place all of the ingredients in a blender. Cover and blend until smooth.
2. Pour into another container and place in the refrigerator. Chill for at least one hour before serving. Makes two servings.

Tropical Isle Fruit Kabobs

Things You'll Need:
6-inch kabob skewers
knife (parent only)
cutting board
Ingredients:
1 papaya
1 mango

1 kiwi
1 banana
1 pineapple
1 (8-ounce) container vanilla yogurt
1 teaspoon coconut extract

Directions:

1. Peel and slice fruits.
2. Slide pieces of fruit onto skewers and refrigerate. (If not serving until later, dip the banana in watered-down lemon juice to prevent discoloration.)
3. Stir coconut extract into vanilla yogurt.
4. Serve your kabobs with coconut dip as you discuss the tropical isles.

Field of Lupine Cookies

Things You'll Need:
3 bowls
cookie sheet
wooden spoon
wax paper
Ingredients:
1 package prepared sugar cookie dough
blue, purple, and rose-colored food coloring

Directions:

1. Separate prepared sugar cookie dough into three sections; place in bowls.

2. With a wooden spoon, mix one color of food coloring with each dough ball. Stir and knead to thoroughly combine.

3. Using one color of dough at a time, pinch off small sections of the dough and press together in the shape of lupines on a cookie sheet.

4. Bake according to package directions; be sure to watch closely because the dough sections are small and will cook quickly.

5. Remove the field of lupines from the cookie sheet to the wax paper.

Sensational Seeds

Things You'll Need:
measuring cups
glass measuring cup
spoon
large bowl
measuring spoons
Ingredients:
6 cups popped popcorn (3 cups unpopped popcorn kernels)
3/4 cup sunflower seeds
1/2 cup raisins
1/2 cup peanut butter
1 tablespoon butter

Directions:

1. Place peanut butter and butter in a glass measuring cup; heat in microwave on low power to melt. Stir to combine.

2. Place popped popcorn in a large bowl.
3. Add sunflower seeds, raisins, and melted peanut butter mixture and mix well.

ART ADVENTURES

Faraway Places Map

Things You'll Need:
small world map
cardboard
white glue
scissors (parent only)
black marker
small star stickers

Directions:

1. Glue a small map of the world to a piece of cardboard. Let dry thoroughly.
2. Cut the map into five sections. Outline each section with a black marker.
3. Put the map together for the children. Then separate the pieces and ask them to put it together again. Point out the places Miss Rumphius visited.
4. Place a star on a tropical isle, on a tall mountain range, on a jungle, and on a desert.

Shell Scenes

Things You'll Need:
shell macaroni
food coloring
resealable plastic bags
white glue
sand
blue construction paper

Directions:

1. Divide shell macaroni into several resealable plastic bags. Drop a couple of drops of food coloring into each bag (blue for water, yellow for the sand, red for the sun) and shake. Set aside to dry for 24 hours.
2. Put some glue at the bottom of a piece of blue construction paper. Cover with a light sprinkling of sand.
3. Glue the colored shell macaroni to the construction paper to create a beach scene.

Flower Garden

Things You'll Need:
blue, purple, and rose-colored construction
    paper
white glue
popsicle sticks
egg carton
play dough
child safety scissors

Directions:

1. Tear sheets of construction paper into small pieces.
2. Glue several small blue pieces of construction paper to one popsicle stick, several purple pieces to another popsicle stick, and several rose-colored pieces to another popsicle stick to form lupines.
3. Cut the top off an egg carton. Put play dough in the holes of the egg carton and stick the popsicle stick "lupines" into the play dough for your own lupine garden.

Mini-Conservatory

Things You'll Need:
small glass container with a lid
dirt
small tropical plants

Directions:

1. Place dirt in the bottom of a glass container.
2. Plant small tropical plants in dirt. Water according to plant directions.
3. Place the lid on top of container and watch the mini-conservatory grow.

Favorite Things

With God all things are possible.
Matthew 19:26

READ...

By: Jan Karon
Published by: Augsburg Books

MISS FANNIE IS A ninety-nine-year-old lady. She is very, very small, almost the same size as a little girl. Miss Fannie lives with her daughter, Miss Wanda, who helps take care of her. Miss Wanda fixes her mama's breakfast, washes her hair, and takes her to church. Miss Fannie has lots and lots of hats: green ones with feathers, red ones with beads, black ones with flowers. But her most favorite hat of all is her pink straw hat with the silk roses, her Easter hat. When asked by her pastor, Miss Fannie unselfishly agrees to give her most prized hat to her church for a fund-raiser. And in giving such a special gift, Miss Fannie receives an unexpected reward.

TEACHING TIPS

Miss Fannie has lots of hats, and each one is her favorite. Miss Fannie was asked to choose a hat to give to the church to help raise money to repair the church building. In choosing to give her favorite Easter Sunday morning hat, she gave up something she really loved. Jesus tells us to help others. He says that when we do something nice for others in his name we are actually doing something nice for him.

Talk about how Miss Fannie made a difference, and how her gift became a special surprise that was given back to her. Ask your children about their favorite things. Discuss things they could do or ways they could give to help your church or your community.

RECIPES

Hats Off

Things You'll Need:
cutting board
serrated knife (parent only)
wax paper
3-inch round cookie cutter
1-inch round cookie cutter
2 small bowls
Ingredients:
1 prepared pound cake
several colors of tube frosting
assorted edible candy flowers and decorative
    candies

Directions:
1. Placing pound cake on wax paper, slice cake in 1-inch thick slices.
2. Taking one 1-inch slice of cake, use the large round cookie cutter to cut a circle.
3. Taking another 1-inch slice of cake, use the smaller round cookie cutter to cut another circle.
4. Using the tube frosting as glue, place the smaller cake round in the top middle of the larger cake round, affixing the two together to form cake "hat."

5. Using the tube frosting as glue, decorate the brim of the hat with edible candy flowers and decorative candies. Makes 6-8 hats.

Miss Fannie's Breakfast Balls with Jelly Dip

Things You'll Need:
skillet
paper towel
wax paper
spoon
measuring cups
cookie sheet

Ingredients:
1/2 pound ground turkey sausage (or you can use bacon that has been cooked in the microwave and crumbled)
1 (8-count) package crescent rolls
1/2 cup cheddar cheese, grated
strawberry jelly
optional: small pieces of vegetables or fruits

Directions:
1. In a skillet, brown sausage until thoroughly cooked. Drain and pat with paper towel to get rid of any excess grease. (This step can be done the night before. Refrigerate cooked and drained sausage in a covered container.)
2. Remove crescent rolls from the package; place on a sheet of wax paper.

3. Place a spoonful of cooked sausage and a spoonful of grated cheese in the center of each piece of dough.

4. Roll dough into a ball and place ball on a cookie sheet. Bake according to package directions.

5. Melt strawberry jelly in microwave for 20 seconds on medium power. Serve as dip with the breakfast balls.

6. Optional: decorate cooked breakfast balls with faces using small pieces of vegetables or fruits. Purchase an additional package of crescent rolls and cut hat shapes from the dough. Bake "hats" according to package directions and serve on top of your vegetable-faced breakfast balls.

Handsome Young Preacher's Tie

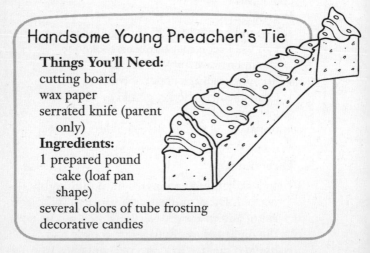

Things You'll Need:
cutting board
wax paper
serrated knife (parent
    only)
Ingredients:
1 prepared pound
    cake (loaf pan
    shape)
several colors of tube frosting
decorative candies

Directions:

1. Cut the loaf pan pound cake horizontally into two pieces. Place on wax paper.

2. Out of one layer of cake cut the length of the tie, a long straight cut starting smaller at the top and flaring to the entire width of the cake at the bottom. Out of the other layer cut two triangles (one for the "knot"; one for the "tip" of the tie). Place one triangle (point down) above the straight piece that is flared at the bottom; with the other triangle, create the tip at the bottom of the tie.
3. Decorate the tie with frosting and decorative candies.

Stained Glass Window Pizzas

Things You'll Need:
medium bowl
rolling pin
wax paper
cookie sheet
knife (parent only)
plastic knife
cutting board
spatula
measuring spoons
measuring cups
Ingredients:
1 package prepared sugar cookie dough
1/4 cup powdered sugar
2 cups various fruits (raspberries, blueberries, kiwi, mandarin oranges, pineapple)
1 tablespoon apple jelly, melted

Directions:

1. Place wax paper on a clean work surface. With rolling pin, roll out sugar cookie dough to about a 3/8-inch thickness.
2. Using a plastic knife, cut out the shape of a church stained glass window (pointed at the top and squared off at the bottom, similar to the shape of a boat).
3. Place the "windows" onto the cookie sheet and bake according to package directions.
4. While cookie "windows" are baking, cut various fruits into small pieces and place in a medium bowl. Add melted apple jelly to fruit and mix.
6. After cookie "windows" have cooled, place them on wax paper and sprinkle lightly with powdered sugar.
7. Arrange fruit mixture on top of the cookie to resemble a stained glass window.

ART ADVENTURES

Miss Fannie's Famous Pink Straw Hat with Silk Roses

Things You'll Need:
straw hat or old hat
pink netting
yellow and pink silk roses
glue gun (adults only) or white glue

Directions:

1. Glue silk flowers around the hat band.
2. Cover the hat with pink netting and glue in place.

Glamorous Gloves

Things You'll Need:
white cotton gloves
fabric glue
paint smocks
beads, lace, sequins, and fabric paints

Directions:

1. Give each child a pair of gloves.
2. Using fabric glue, have each child decorate gloves with beads, buttons, sequins, and fabric paints.

Jazzy Jackets

Things You'll Need:
white butcher paper
marker
child safety scissors
paint smocks
washable squirt paints
white glue
buttons

Directions:

1. Roll out the butcher paper and ask each child to lie down on the paper.
2. Trace around the child's head and upper body with the marker.
3. Cut the form out of the butcher paper. Have each child decorate his or her jacket using washable squirt paints and buttons.

Hat Boxes

You will need:
small hat boxes (found at craft stores)
buttons, bows, ribbons, and sequins
pink silk flower petals
stickers
markers
white glue

Directions:
Have children decorate the hat boxes using
  various art supplies.

Easter Tree

Things You'll Need:
2 cups flour
1 cup salt
1 cup cold water
large bowl
food coloring

white acrylic paint
plastic resealable storage bags
wax paper
rolling pin
cookie cutters (cross, dove, angels, and lily)
plastic drinking straw
plastic wrap
ribbon
sturdy branch
molding clay
artificial Easter grass
container

Directions:

1. In a large bowl, sift flour and salt. Add water. Knead the mixture until it forms a medium-stiff, smooth dough. If necessary, add more flour to stiffen the dough.

2. Divide dough into several balls. Working little dabs of food coloring into each ball, color each dough ball a different color. (For white dough mix in white acrylic paint.) Store colored dough in plastic bags in the refrigerator until you are ready to make Easter ornaments.

3. Place a sheet of wax paper on a clean surface. Dust a small amount of flour onto the wax paper.

4. Using a rolling pin, roll out the dough to a 1/2-inch thickness. Dip cookie cutters in flour, then place down on dough to cut out shapes. (If you cannot find Christian Easter

symbols, make a master pattern from cardboard and cut around the shape with a kitchen knife.)

5. Once each shape has been cut out, insert the drinking straw about 1/2 inch down from the top of the shape. Remove straw. This will form a hole in the ornament for ribbon to be tied through.

6. Place shapes on a cookie sheet and dry them in a 325-degree oven for one to two hours or until they feel hard to the touch.

7. While cookies are drying, place molding clay into a container. Insert the branch into the clay and cover the clay with artificial grass.

8. Tie ribbon through cooled ornaments and hang from branches of the "tree."

caterpillar Capers

Anyone who believes in Christ is a new creation.
The old has gone! The new has come!
2 Corinthians 5:17

READ...

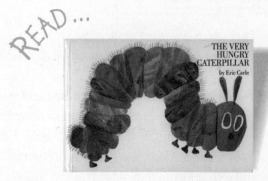

By: Eric Carle
Published by: Philomel Books

BY THE LIGHT OF the moon, an egg is laid on a leaf. As the sun comes up, the egg hatches and out pops a very tiny, very hungry caterpillar. To ease his hunger, the caterpillar eats his way through a different type of fruit each day. When Saturday rolls around, the caterpillar is still very hungry and just a bit out of control. He eats through a combination of sweet, sour, and greasy foods and winds up with an upset stomach. To help his stomachache go away, the caterpillar eats a nice green leaf and realizes he is not hungry anymore. And he is no longer little. He is a big fat caterpillar, ready to build a cocoon. When the once very small caterpillar emerges from his cocoon, he is a big and beautiful butterfly.

TEACHING TIPS

The Very Hungry Caterpillar provides many angles for teaching: counting, the days of the week, and various foods. The most unique concept is how God creates an egg to become a caterpillar and how that caterpillar becomes a butterfly. Discuss how, just as he created the caterpillar, God created people. As we learn more about God, we grow and change to become more like him.

Call 1-800-LIVE-BUGS to order a caterpillar kit. Or order a butterfly garden by Insect Lore (about $20.00 through educational toy, novelty, and nature stores) or through the Internet at www.sci-encestuff.com. It comes with a coupon to redeem for caterpillars, a colorful butterfly house, a feeding kit, instructions, and additional butterfly information.

RECIPES

Caterpillar Cookies

Things You'll Need:
cookie sheet
large bowl
large spoon
measuring cups
Ingredients:
1 box Duncan Hines sugar cookie mix
yellow food coloring
1 (6-ounce) bag miniature chocolate chips

Directions:
1. Preheat oven to 350 degrees.
2. Prepare dough according to cookie package directions, adding yellow food coloring to the liquid ingredients.
3. Roll four small balls of dough and arrange on the cookie sheet to resemble a caterpillar. Make as many "caterpillars" as you can with the dough.

4. Press two miniature chocolate chips into the ball on one end of each caterpillar to simulate caterpillar eyes.
5. Bake according to package directions.

Caterpillar Fruit Salad

Things You'll Need:
Styrofoam egg carton cut in half lengthwise
pipe cleaners
hole punch
Ingredients:
several flavors of yogurt
apples, sliced
bananas, sliced
strawberries, sliced
optional: cut-up vegetables and ranch-
    flavored dip

Directions:
1. Using a hole punch, punch a hole in each side of the first compartment of the egg carton.
2. Give each child two pipe cleaners and show them how to insert the pipe cleaner into the punched holes to form the caterpillar's antennae.
3. Fill the first three compartments of the egg carton with washed, sliced fruits.
4. Fill the last three compartments of the egg carton with your favorite flavored yogurt. Dip the fruits into the yogurt for a great caterpillar snack.

5. Optional: Try this with cut-up vegetables and ranch-flavored dip.

Popcorn Caterpillar

Things You'll Need:
large bowl
wax paper
large spoon
large microwave-safe bowl
Ingredients:
1/4 cup butter
1 16-ounce bag marshmallows
12 cups popped popcorn (6 cups unpopped popcorn kernels)
pretzel sticks
M&Ms
red string licorice

Directions:

1. Place butter and marshmallows in a microwave-safe bowl. Microwave on high for 1 1/2 to 2 minutes, or until marshmallows are melted.
2. Remove marshmallows from the microwave. Stir the mixture with a spoon until thoroughly combined.
3. Place popped popcorn in a large bowl. Pour melted marshmallows over popcorn. Let cool.
4. Rub butter on both hands. Take some of the covered popcorn and form four small balls.

Line the balls up to form the body of a
caterpillar.
5. Place the caterpillar sculpture on a serving
plate. Add pretzel sticks for antennae, M&Ms
for eyes, and red licorice for legs.

Wings and Things

Things You'll Need:
serrated knife
  (parent only)
cutting board
small bowls
spoons
plastic knives
Ingredients:
1 prepared pound cake
8 ounces cream cheese or prepared frosting
food coloring
mini M&Ms
miniature chocolate chips
red cinnamon candies
gummy bears

Directions:
1. Divide cream cheese or frosting into four equal
   parts. Place each part in a separate small bowl,
   add food colorings, and blend.
2. Cut the cake into 1-inch slices and then cut the
   slices in half.
3. Place the two points of the butterfly wings
   together on the plate.

4. Using plastic knives, have children spread the colored cream cheese or frosting on the cake surface to create wing patterns.
5. Add other decorations to create more butterfly features.

ART ADVENTURES

Papier Mâché Cocoon

Things You'll Need:
1 (11-inch) balloon
scissors (parent only)
1 roll plaster gauze (available at craft stores)
water
yardstick
bowl
wrapped candies and plastic toy butterflies

Directions:

1. Blow up the balloon, but not too fully. Tie tightly.
2. Measure one yard of plaster gauze. Cut it into three-inch pieces.
3. Dip one piece of plaster gauze in a bowl filled with water. With your fingers, gently squeeze out extra water.
4. Apply gauze strips to the balloon by flattening each piece, then smoothing it with your hands. (Do not cover the tied area of the balloon.) Let the plaster dry for about 15 minutes.

5. Pop the balloon, then remove it. Fill the "cocoon" with little toy butterflies and wrapped candies and give away as a gift!

Bow Tie Butterflies

Things You'll Need:
bow tie pasta
food coloring
several resealable plastic bags
rubbing alcohol
newspaper
white glue
child safety scissors
construction paper
black marker
tissue paper or pastel-colored cello paper
 (Easter basket paper)

Directions:

One day ahead of art project:

1. Place ten pieces of bow tie pasta each into four separate plastic bags. Add 1 teaspoon of rubbing alcohol and a drop or two of food coloring (a different color for each plastic bag). Shake thoroughly to evenly distribute the color.

2. Place colored bow tie pasta on newspaper to dry.

Day of activity:

3. Give each child a large piece of construction paper and some glue. Ask the child to glue different bow tie (butterfly) colors to the surface of the paper. Add antennae to each butterfly with the black marker.

4. Cut flower shapes from the tissue paper or cello paper and glue around the butterflies. Cut flower stems and leaves from construction paper and glue under the tissue paper flowers.

Balloon Butterflies

Things You'll Need:
balloons
large doilies
child safety scissors
Scotch tape
black construction paper
black marker

Directions:

1. Cut doilies in half or into the shape of butterfly wings.

2. Blow up several balloons and give one to each child.

3. Tape "wings" to either side of the balloon.

4. Cut 1/2-inch by 5-inch strips from black construction paper and tape to the front of the balloon to form antennae.

5. Using black marker, carefully mark out butterfly eyes on the balloon.

Colorful Wings

Things You'll Need:
10-inch paper plates
child safety scissors
various colors of tissue paper
spray bottle filled with water

Directions:

1. Cut paper plate into the shape of a butterfly.
2. Tear various colors of tissue paper into strips.
3. Spray paper plate with water; lay strips of tissue paper over the wet paper plate. Let dry.
4. Remove strips of tissue to see colorful butterfly wings.

Clothespin Butterflies

Things You'll Need:
2 square paper napkins
scissors
markers or crayons
white glue
variety of decorative suppies: buttons, sequins,
    stickers, confetti
clothespin
pipe cleaner
small refrigerator magnet

Directions:

1. Fold first paper napkin in half, forming eight layers, to make the large wings.
2. Fold second napkin into thirds to make a smaller, thicker set of wings.
3. Decorate tops of "wings" and clothespin with markers or crayons. Add special decorative touches with sequins, small buttons, and confetti.
4. Placing some glue between the clothespin prongs, gather and slide the larger paper wings between the clothespin prongs.
5. Slide the smaller set of wings into place on top of the larger wings.
6. Twist a pipe cleaner around the neck of the clothespin for antennae.
7. Glue a magnet to the back side of the butterfly for a great refrigerator magnet.

Critter Jitters

God . . . made all kinds of creatures that move
along the ground. . . . and God saw that it was
good.

Genesis 1:25

READ . . .

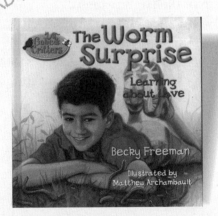

By: Becky Freeman
Published by: Chariot Victor Books

IN THIS STORY, A warm-hearted, critter-crazy little boy named Gabe tries to find his mother the perfect critter birthday gift. Gabe searches everywhere for a quiet critter with a pretty pattern on its back because he knows his mother loves quiet moments and pretty things. Gabe gets discouraged because his older brothers and sister already have Mom's presents wrapped and on the kitchen table—so he tries harder and harder to find his gift for his mother. The snapping turtle was pretty and quiet, but it bit something awful. The beautiful bluebird was fancy, but it was a mother too, and Gabe knew her baby birds loved her too much to take her away from them. Finally he decides upon some wiggly-squiggly worms as his gift, and his mother is certainly surprised.

TEACHING TIPS

Working hard, like Gabe did, to find a gift that really shows your love makes the gift much more meaningful.

There are many ways you can help your children show their love for their mother. One great way is by helping them make a coupon book. Coupons can be good for "one free room cleaning without complaining," "an undisturbed Saturday morning," or "a night out with friends, without coming home to a messy house."

Discuss with your children the best gifts they have ever received. Use this opportunity to talk about God's love for us and others, and about the greatest gift of all, God's gift to us: Jesus.

RECIPES

Wiggle Squiggly Worm Biscuits with Mud Butter

Things You'll Need:
cookie sheet
small microwave-safe bowl
Ingredients:
1 can refrigerated breadsticks
1/2 stick margarine, softened
1 cup chocolate chips
powdered sugar, to taste

Directions:
1. Separate the breadsticks; place on cookie sheet.
2. Twist and curve each breadstick into shape of a slithering worm.
3. Bake according to package directions.
4. While "worms" are baking, microwave chocolate chips in 40-second intervals for 2 minutes, or until melted. Set aside until cool.
5. Stir cooled chocolate chip mixture into softened margarine; sprinkle in a little powdered sugar to taste.

6. Serve melted chocolate chip mixture as "mud" with breadstick "worms" for a disgusting treat.

Salted Bird Feathers

Things You'll Need:
medium glass bowl
measuring cup
measuring spoons
large spoon
cookie sheet
resealable plastic bag
cooking spray
Ingredients:
1 (1 1/2-2 pound) package of chicken wings
1 cup buttermilk
1 cup flour
1 teaspoon salt
1/2 teaspoon pepper
1/2 teaspoon paprika

Directions:

1. Preheat oven to 350 degrees.
2. Place chicken wings in a bowl. Pour buttermilk over wings and stir to coat.
3. Place flour, salt, pepper, and paprika into resealable plastic bag. Using tongs, pick wings out of buttermilk and add them to the bag. Seal bag and shake.
4. Spray cookie sheet with cooking spray. Place coated wings onto the cookie sheet.
5. Bake for 15 minutes; turn and bake an additional 15 minutes. Makes 6–8 servings.

Snappy Turtles

Things You'll Need:
paper plate
plastic knife
Ingredients:
Ritz crackers
peanut butter
raisins
optional: vanilla wafers, peanut butter,
   M&Ms

Directions:

1. Spread a Ritz cracker with peanut butter for the body of the turtle.
2. Place one raisin for the turtle's head, four raisins for the turtle's feet, and one for the turtle's tail. (Place so the raisins are partially beyond the edge of the cracker.)
3. Top the "turtle" with the second Ritz cracker. Raisins should show between the two crackers.
4. Optional: Try vanilla wafers and peanut butter, with M&Ms for the turtle's legs, head, and tail.

Critter Fritters

Things You'll Need:
3 small microwave-safe bowls
spoons
wax paper
little bowls for sprinkles
Ingredients:
1 bag animal crackers

2 cups vanilla baking chips
various colors of food coloring
colorful sprinkles

Directions:
1. Divide vanilla baking chips into three bowls. Microwave on medium heat, stirring in 30-second intervals, until melted.
2. Place one drop of food coloring into each bowl (a different color per bowl); stir to thoroughly mix in color.
3. Dip end of each animal cracker into colored, melted chips and then into favorite sprinkles. Place on wax paper to dry.

Peanut Butter and Jelly Fudge

Things You'll Need:
heavy saucepan
spoon
measuring cups
measuring spoons
9-inch square glass pan
microwave-safe bowl
squirt bottle
Ingredients:
3/4 cup butter
2 cups brown sugar
2/3 cup evaporated milk
1 (10-ounce) bag peanut butter morsels
1 teaspoon vanilla extract
1 (7-ounce) jar marshmallow cream

1/2 cup seedless raspberry jelly
optional: crushed potato chips and pickle
   slices

Directions:

1. In a heavy saucepan, combine butter, sugar, and milk. Bring to a boil, stirring constantly. Reduce heat and simmer for 5 minutes.
2. Stir in peanut butter morsels, vanilla, and marshmallow cream. Remove from heat and stir until all is melted.
3. Pour into a lightly greased 9-inch square pan. Cool.
4. Place jelly in a microwave-safe bowl and microwave for 30 seconds, or until melted. Fill squirt bottle with cooled jelly and squirt jelly over the peanut butter fudge.
5. Optional: Top with crushed potato chips and pickle slices!

Art Adventures

Worm Paintings

Things You'll Need:
plastic wiggly fishing worms
kite string
scissors (parent only)
various colors of tempera paint
paint smocks
small bowls
white butcher paper

Directions:

1. Cut a 6-inch piece of kite string and tie it to a plastic wiggly fishing worm.
2. Pour different colored paints into small bowls.
3. Roll out a piece of butcher paper on a clean work surface.
4. Dip worms into the paints and drag them across the butcher paper.

Thumbprint Critters

Things You'll Need:
yellow construction paper
paint smocks
various colors of tempera paint
small bowls or cleaned butter tubs
markers

Directions:

1. Pour paints into small containers or bowls.
2. Stick thumbs into the different colors of paint and make prints on the yellow construction paper. (Use green paint for turtles, blue for birds, gray for doodle bugs, brown for worms.)
3. Once thumbprints are dry, use markers to create critters by drawing legs, feathers, and little feet.

Turtle-riffic

Things You'll Need:
child safety scissors
green construction
    paper
white glue
decorative
    wiggly eyes
heavy paper bowl
markers

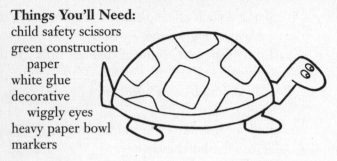

Directions:

1. Use scissors to cut turtle's legs, head, and tail from a piece of green construction paper.
2. Glue wiggly eyes onto the turtle's head.
3. Turn the bowl upside down and glue legs, head, and tail, to the underside rim of the bowl. Let dry.
4. Use markers to make big squares on the turtle's back; then color.

Doodle Bug Highways

Things You'll Need:
white butcher paper
brown paint or gooey mud
paint brush
paint smocks
child safety scissors
yarn
gray modeling clay
glue

Directions:

1. Place white butcher paper on work surface. Using a paint brush, paint butcher paper with brown paint or gooey mud.
2. Run index finger all through the brown paint or mud to form doodle bug highways. Set aside to dry.
3. Cut 1-inch pieces of yarn and fray.
4. Form little balls with gray modeling clay. Stick short pieces of frayed yarn underneath each ball for the doodle bugs' legs.
5. Glue doodle bugs to the highways.

Bluebirds' Nest

Things You'll Need:
3/4 cup salt
2 cups flour
3/4 cup water
1/2 teaspoon alum
plastic bowl
garlic press
paintbrushes
red and blue tempera paints
hot glue gun (adults only)
leaves
grass
straw
sturdy branch

Directions:

1. Prepare salt clay by mixing salt, flour, and alum in a plastic bowl; add water gradually. When the dough is thoroughly mixed, knead about ten times, adding more water if it is too dry.
2. Place small amounts of the dough in a garlic press, squeezing dough through the press to form "straw" for the birds' nest. Continue process until you have enough "straw" to make a nest. Form nest and set it aside.
3. Form a bird out of remaining dough. (When the dough is dry, paint the bird blue with a red tummy.)
4. When nest is dry, hot glue (adults only) the nest to a tree branch. Fill the nest with leaves, grass, and straw. Place the bluebird in the nest.

Alphabet Alley

May the words of my mouth and the thoughts of
my heart be pleasing in your eyes.
Psalm 19:14

READ...

Chicka Chicka ABC

By: Bill Martin Jr. and John Archambault
Published by: Simon and Schuster

79

DO ALPHABETS CLIMB TREES? They do in *Chicka Chicka ABC*. B follows A and C follows B right up the coconut tree. This brightly illustrated book walks the youngest reader right up the tree with the alphabet, offering a great lesson on the sequencing of letters. Once the entire twenty-six letters climb the coconut tree, the tree collapses, spilling the alphabet all over the ground.

TEACHING TIPS

This colorful book is just right for the younger preschool child. Once you have enjoyed the book several times, try going back through the book on a letter hunt. On your hunt, find the letters that spell your children's first names.

Purchase an alphabet puzzle or cut out letters from construction paper. Lay the alphabet out on the floor and ask your child to find the letters that spell his or her first name.

Try looking up the meaning of your child's name: Sarah, for example, means *princess*. If your child's name was chosen for a special reason, explain to your child how his or her name was chosen.

RECIPES

Alphabet Cupcakes

Things You'll Need:
large bowl
electric mixer
measuring cups
12-hole cupcake pan
12 paper cupcake liners
Ingredients:
1 prepared cake mix
several colors of prepared tube frosting

Directions:

1. Preheat oven according to package directions.
2. Prepare cake mix according to package directions; pour into cupcake tin lined with baking papers. Bake according to package directions.
3. After cupcakes have cooled, frost and decorate each cupcake around a letter of the alphabet: *A* could be a cupcake decorated to resemble an airplane; *B*, decorated as a bumble bee; *C*, decorated as a cat, etc.

ABC Pancakes

Things You'll Need:
griddle
spatula
large spoon

small spoon
Ingredients:
1 box pancake mix or favorite pancake
   recipe
syrup
fresh fruit

Directions:

1. Prepare your favorite pancake batter.
2. Using a small spoon, pour batter in the shape of a letter onto hot griddle or skillet. (The letter will have to be made backward on the skillet in order to look right when pancake is served.)
3. When the bottom side of the letter is browned, use a large spoon to pour more batter over the letter shape.
4. Continue to bake until the pancake is done.
3. Serve with favorite fruit and syrup.

Alphabet Snack Attack

Things You'll Need:
large resealable plastic bag
measuring cups
2 cups alphabet cereal
1 cup raisins
1/2 cup dried apricots
1/2 cup dried bananas

Directions:

Place all ingredients in a resealable plastic
   bag and shake to combine.

ART ADVENTURES

Name Cheer

Things You'll Need:
big paper letters of the alphabet (found in
  school supply stores)
pictures cut from magazines
child safety scissors
white glue
butcher paper

Directions:

1. Pick out—or let your child pick out—the letters that spell your child's name. Glue the child's name in a straight vertical line on a long sheet of butcher paper.
2. Using your child's name as an acrostic, create a cheer (e.g., *Sarah* could be: Super, Awesome, Remarkable, Adorable, Hugs)
3. Explain the words being used to create the cheer. Cut pictures out of magazines that match each word and glue next to the appropriate letter of the acrostic on the butcher paper.

Letter of the Day

Things You'll Need:
1 1/4 cups flour

3/4 cup cinnamon
1 cup salt
1 cup water
alphabet cookie cutters
large bowl
paint smocks
measuring cups
wax paper
various colors of tempera paint
stickers

Directions:

1. Preheat oven to 300 degrees.
2. Prepare spice salt dough recipe by mixing together flour, cinnamon, salt, and water. Knead thoroughly to combine.
3. Place on a cinnamon sprinkled work surface and roll dough out. Cut out the alphabet from the dough with the cookie cutters.
4. Bake 25 to 30 minutes. Let cool before decorating.
5. Decorate letters with paints and stickers. (Use stickers whose first letter begins with the letter they are being stuck to: for *A* use apple stickers; for *B*, bumble bee stickers, and so on.)
6. Hang a "letter of the day" on the door or wall.
7. Other options: Make your child's name. Stick with heavy double stick tape to the child's bedroom door. Or glue little magnets to the back of each letter to create a refrigerator spelling game.

Paper Coconut Trees

Things You'll Need:
small brown paper bag
green tissue paper
brown tissue paper
white glue
orange construction
   paper
alphabet stickers

Directions:

1. Twist a small brown paper
    bag to form a tree trunk.
2. Once tree trunk is formed,
    tear pieces down from the top
    of the bag to form the branches. Glue the tree
    to an orange piece of construction paper.
3. Tear long sheets of green tissue paper to form
    long fronds found on a coconut tree. Glue
    these to the top of the brown bag.
4. Tear brown tissue paper into strips and wad
    them into small balls to form coconuts for the
    tree. Glue those under the tree leaves.
5. Stick alphabet stickers underneath and all
    around the tree.

Silly Willys

How you made me is amazing and wonderful. I praise you for that.

Psalm 139:14

READ ...

By: Jamie Lee Curtis
Published by: HarperCollins

SILLY, CRANKY, EXCITED, OR happy—everyone has moods that change each day. *Today I Feel Silly and Other Moods That Make My Day* looks at the wild and zany moods a young girl feels as she lives her life with its ups and downs. We experience her moods with her as she eats pancakes for dinner and spaghetti for breakfast, as she burns her cocoa and has a fight with her best friend, as she has friends sleeping over and a new sibling on the way. The book is full of amusing stories, creating a fun look at life for parent and child alike.

TEACHING TIPS

Help your children explore and identify their moods. Ask them to make faces that represent the many moods people experience: How do you look when you are mad? How do you look when you are happy? What is your best surprised face? Once a specific mood is identified, talk about how one feels during that particular mood. This is a great way to get your children to discuss how they feel, when they felt a certain way, and how they feel today.

RECIPES

Nutty Noodles

Things You'll Need:
2 glass bowls

whisk
measuring cup
measuring spoons
2 forks
Ingredients:
variety of favorite fresh vegetables
1 (8-ounce) box thin noodles
1/3 cup peanut butter
2/3 cup hot water
3 tablespoons soy sauce
1 tablespoon cider vinegar
1/2 teaspoon minced garlic

Directions:
1. Cook noodles according to package directions.
2. Cut up vegetables and place in a glass bowl. Add 2 tablespoons water, cover loosely, and microwave on high for 2 minutes.
3. While microwaving vegetables, mix peanut butter and hot water; stir until creamy. Add soy sauce, cider vinegar, and garlic; stir thoroughly.
4. Toss noodles and steamed vegetables with sauce. Makes 2 servings.

Super Silly Pancakes

Things You'll Need:
cookie sheet
spatula
small bowls
spoon
individual plates

Ingredients:
1 box frozen pancakes
1 can whipped cream
variety of favorite fruits, sliced

Directions:

1. Cook pancakes according to package directions. Let cool.
2. Give each child a pancake.
3. Squirt a layer of whipping cream on top of the pancake and smooth out with the back of a spoon.
4. Have child select favorite fruits to make faces on the pancakes that match his or her mood.

Easy Icy Cream

Things You'll Need:
large bowl
large spoon
1 (13-ounce) coffee can with tight-fitting lid
1 (39-ounce) coffee can with tight-fitting lid
duct tape
5–6 cups crushed ice
1/2–1 cup rock salt or ice cream salt
Ingredients:
1 cup whole milk
1 cup heavy cream
1/2 cup sugar
1 teaspoon vanilla
pinch of salt
optional: 1/2 cup chopped fruit or 1/4 cup crushed candy bars

Directions:

1. Pour milk and cream into a large bowl and stir.
2. Add sugar, salt, and vanilla to mixture and mix well.
3. Add optional ingredients, if desired, and mix well.
4. Pour mixture into small coffee can; fill until two inches from top.
5. Snap on lid; seal with duct tape to reduce leaks.
6. Place small can inside larger can.
7. Fill space between two cans, alternating 1 cup ice and 2 tablespoons rock salt, until full to top.
8. Place lid on large can; seal lid with tape to prevent leaks.
9. Ask children to roll the can nonstop along a sidewalk, patio, or other level area for about 20 minutes.
10. Open can carefully to prevent spilling; rinse off inside can before removing duct tape to keep salt out of the ice cream. Makes 4 servings.

Lemonade Cookies

Things You'll Need:
food processor or large plastic bag with rolling pin
large bowl
measuring cup
large spoon
teaspoon
airtight container
Ingredients:

1 box vanilla wafers
1 (6-ounce) can frozen lemonade, thawed
2 cups powdered sugar
1 stick margarine, melted and cooled

Directions:

1. Crush vanilla wafers in a food processor, or put in a large plastic bag and roll with a rolling pin until finely crushed.
2. In a large bowl, combine crushed wafers, lemonade, powdered sugar, and melted margarine. Stir thoroughly.
3. Let mixture stand for about 30 minutes.
4. Scoop out mixture with a teaspoon and roll into balls.
5. Store in an airtight container until ready to serve.

French Braids

Things You'll Need:
cookie sheet
large spoon
small bowl
measuring cup
pastry brush
Ingredients:
2 cans refrigerated breadsticks
1/2 stick margarine, melted
1/4 cup sugar
1/2 teaspoon cinnamon
various decorative sprinkles

Directions:

1. Separate breadsticks and group two by two on a clean work surface.
2. Twist breadsticks to form a braid; place on a cookie sheet.
3. Place sugar in a small bowl; add cinnamon and mix.
4. Using a pastry brush, brush "French braids" with melted margarine; and sprinkle with sugar/cinnamon mixture.
5. Top with decorative sprinkles and bake according to package directions.

ART ADVENTURES

I'm a Star

Things You'll Need:
construction paper
child safety scissors
glitter
white glue
yarn
decorative wiggly eyes

Directions:

1. Cut construction paper into the shape of a large star.
2. Decorate the star with a face and hair to resemble your favorite mood.

Silly Cookie Bags

Things You'll Need:
brown paper lunch bags
markers
white glue
ribbons
buttons
sequins
stickers
yarn
glitter

Directions:

1. Using all sorts of art supplies, decorate the bags. Set aside to dry.
2. Optional: Fill bags with cookies for an "excited" day bake sale.

Fancy Faces

Things You'll Need:
shirt cardboards or poster board
child safety scissors
popsicle sticks
glue
markers

Directions:

1. Cut two circles out of the shirt cardboards or poster board.

2. Using markers, decorate one circle with a happy face, the other circle with a sad face.
3. Glue the circles to either side of the popsicle stick, decorated side out. Set aside to dry.

Super Silly Spaghetti Scenes

Things You'll Need:
1 package spaghetti
several colors of tempera paints
small bowls
heavy white construction paper
paint smocks

Directions:

1. Cook spaghetti according to package directions. Drain and cool.
2. Give each child a piece of construction paper.
3. Dip individual pieces of spaghetti into the paint and brush them over the construction paper to create painted designs.

Imagination Station

Every animal in the forest already belongs to me.
And so do the cattle on a thousand hills.
Psalm 50:10

READ...

By: Maurice Sendak
Published by: HarperCollins

LITTLE MAX GETS INTO all kinds of mischief when he is wearing his wolf suit. Finally, he gets into things so much that his mother calls him a "wild thing." After Max talks back to his mother, he is sent to his room without eating his supper. While in his room, still in his wolf suit, Max's imagination takes him on adventures in his private boat over the ocean and far, far away, to a place where the "wild things" are. The wild things try their best to scare him, but Max tames them with a magic trick. He instantly becomes their king, until, of course, he gets homesick and hungry and sails back home to his room.

TEACHING TIPS

Where the Wild Things Are explores the fabulous imagination inherent in all children. Take this opportunity to play imaginary games. Help your child create a "private boat" story of their own, asking questions that will fuel their imagination. What would they do on their faraway island? Who would they meet?

RECIPES

"Wild Things" Claws

Things You'll Need:
cookie sheet

spatula
2 small glass bowls
measuring cups
measuring spoons
tablespoon
Ingredients:
1 can large refrigerator biscuits
1/2 stick margarine, melted
1/2 cup sugar
1 teaspoon cinnamon
1 jar strawberry preserves
1 package sliced almonds

Directions:

1. Place sugar and cinnamon in a small bowl; stir to combine.
2. Place each biscuit in melted margarine; turn to coat. Place margarine-coated biscuit into cinnamon/sugar mixture, then onto a cookie sheet.
3. Using the back of a tablespoon, make a big indention in the biscuit. Fill indention with preserves.
4. For claws, place five almond slices along one side of each biscuit.
5. Bake according to package directions. Makes 8 servings.

Yellow Eyes

Things You'll Need:
paper plates

plastic knives
Ingredients:
vanilla wafers
yellow prepared frosting
miniature chocolate chips

Directions:

1. Place several vanilla wafers on a paper plate.
2. Frost wafers with yellow frosting.
3. Place several miniature chocolate chips in a circle in the center of each frosted wafer to form the outline of the pupil.

"King of the Wild Things" Crown

Things You'll Need:
cookie sheet
cooking spray
small round cookie cutter
measuring cup
pastry brush
knife (parent only)
cutting board
Ingredients:
1 can refrigerator biscuits
1/4 cup dried apricots, chopped
1/4 cup craisins (dried cranberries)
1/4 cup golden raisins
1/4 cup margarine, melted
1/4 cup cinnamon
1/4 cup sugar

Directions:

1. Open the can of biscuits and place on a cookie sheet that has been sprayed with cooking spray.
2. Using a small round cookie cutter, cut the center out of the biscuits.
3. Brush melted margarine over each biscuit.
4. Press dried fruits into biscuits to form the jewels of the crown.
5. Bake biscuits according to package directions.
6. Coat leftover biscuit centers with melted margarine and roll in cinnamon and sugar. Bake according to package directions until golden brown.

Private Boat Pita

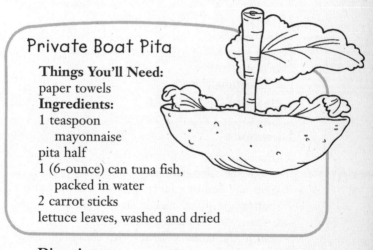

Things You'll Need:
paper towels
Ingredients:
1 teaspoon
  mayonnaise
pita half
1 (6-ounce) can tuna fish,
  packed in water
2 carrot sticks
lettuce leaves, washed and dried

Directions:

1. Use a carrot stick to spread mayonnaise inside one side of pita pocket.

2. Place lettuce leaves on the mayonnaise-coated side of pita.
3. Place tuna fish in front of the lettuce.
4. Place two carrot sticks in the middle of the pita to form the mast of the sailboat.

Banana Boat

Things You'll Need:
plastic knife
paper plates
Ingredients:
1 banana
1 bag large, fat
  pretzel sticks
peanut butter
chocolate chips
minimarshmallows
1 package Fruit by the Foot

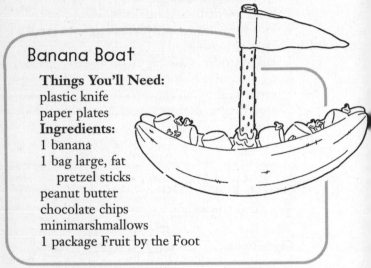

Directions:
1. Peel banana. With knife, cut the center out of the banana lengthwise.
2. Dip one end of a fat pretzel stick into peanut butter and place upright in the middle of the banana, to simulate the mast.
3. Fill in the banana "boat" with chocolate chips and minimarshmallows.
4. Tear off a portion of Fruit by the Foot and wrap it around the pretzel stick to form the sail.

ART ADVENTURES

Monster Masks

Things You'll Need:
2 heavy paper plates
wooden stir stick
stapler
white glue
fabric fur
scissors (parent only)
large yellow buttons
Styrofoam packing pellets

Directions:

1. Place paper plates face-to-face. Slide the paint stirrer into the bottom middle of the plates.
2. Staple around the circumference of the plates to form a "wild thing face."
3. Cut and glue strips of fabric fur to both sides of the face.
4. Cut triangles from fabric fur for ears; staple to the sides of the plates.
5. Glue yellow buttons onto the fur for eyes.
6. Glue Styrofoam packing pellets to the fur face to form the sharp teeth.
7. Once monster mask has dried, have your own "wild thing" rumpus.

Sail Away Sailboats

Things You'll Need:
one sheet of newspaper

Directions:

1. Fold the sheet of newspaper in half by bringing the top half down at the center of the fold.

2. Fold the top two corners down toward the bottom center, leaving about two inches of the bottom edge below the point where the top corners meet.

3. Fold the bottom edges up on each side.

4. Bring the outside corners together, and flatten sideways into a square.

5. Holding the open points toward you, fold the loose corners up to meet each side, forming a triangle.

6. Bring the outside corners together, and flatten sideways into a square.

7. Gently pull the top two loose corners open to form a boat. Let children float the sail away sailboats in a sink or wash tub.

Forest Frolic

Things You'll Need:
4 brown paper lunch bags
child safety scissors
blue construction paper
white glue
aluminum pie plate
green tempera paint
paint smocks

Directions:

1. Cut off bottom of each brown paper bag.
2. Twist bags to form tree trunks.
3. Glue tree trunks down onto the blue construction paper.
4. Pour green paint into a pie plate.
5. Dip fingers into the paint, then paint "leaves" all around the brown paper bag tree trunks.

Ocean in a Bottle

Things You'll Need:
1 (20-ounce) clear plastic soda bottle with twist-off cap
water
1/2 teaspoon blue food coloring
baby oil
miniature plastic sailboat (small enough to fit through the opening of the plastic bottle)

Directions:

1. Pour 1 cup of water into a plastic soda bottle.
2. Add blue food coloring to the bottle.
3. Drop 3 drops of baby oil into the bottle.
4. Place the miniature plastic sailboat into the bottle. Twist the cap back on the bottle. Turn the bottle side to side and watch the "waves" move the sailboat to and fro.

Fall Fun

But the fruit the Holy Spirit produces is love, joy
and peace. It is being patient, kind, and good.
Galatians 5:22

READ ...

By: Liz Curtis Higgs
Published by: Thomas Nelson

The Pumpkin Patch Parable
Written by Liz Curtis Higgs & Illustrated by Nancy Munger
Published by Tommy Nelson™, a division of Thomas Nelson, Inc. © 1995. Used by permission

IN THE HOT SUMMERTIME, the patient farmer plants pumpkins and cares for them as they grow. Finally, the day comes when the pumpkins are ready for harvest. The farmer selects one from which to create his masterpiece. The farmer cuts into the pumpkin and removes all of the insides. Then he carves a smiling face. The light of a small candle inside the carved pumpkin as it illuminates its surroundings is compared to how the heavenly Father grows and changes his people to be a light in the darkness.

TEACHING TIPS

As pumpkins grow they begin to look different from each other. They are all different shapes and sizes. Just like pumpkins, people come in all shapes, sizes, and colors. There are many different types of people and colors of skin, and each color is beautiful. Further, no matter what color we are on the outside, what matters is what is on the inside.

Purchase several different shapes and colors of pumpkins and have a carving party. (Have small children decorate their pumpkins with markers—lots less mess and still fun!) As each person designs a different pumpkin face, discuss how things that make us different also make us special. God made each one of us, and he loves us just as we are.

RECIPES

Roasted Pumpkin Seeds

Things You'll Need:
1 medium pumpkin
paper towel
ice cream scoop
measuring cup
measuring spoons
cookie sheet
Ingredients:
2 cups pumpkin seeds
1 tablespoon oil
1/2 teaspoon salt
1/2 teaspoon cinnamon

Directions:

1. Preheat oven to 350 degrees.
2. Cut pumpkin open and remove pumpkin seeds with an ice cream scoop.
3. Rinse pumpkin seeds and dry on a paper towel.
4. Place dry seeds on a cookie sheet; toss with oil and seasonings.
5. Bake for 20 minutes, tossing every 5 minutes, until golden.

Harvest Hash

Things You'll Need:
small brown lunch bags

white glue
fall-colored silk leaves
raffia or ribbon
large mixing bowl
wooden spoon
Ingredients:
1 box Bugle chips (resemble cornucopia)
1 small bag pumpkin candies or candy corns
2 cups caramel popcorn
1 cup golden raisins
2 cups small pretzels
1 cup peanuts

Directions:

1. Glue several fall-colored silk leaves to the outside of each bag.
2. Place all ingredients in a large bowl; stir thoroughly.
3. Divide mixture evenly into decorated bags.
4. Tie each bag with raffia and attach an "I'm thankful for you" note.

Scarecrow Hand

Things You'll Need:
large bowl
plastic glove
raffia
plastic toy ring
measuring cups
Ingredients:
1 small bag candy corn

1 cup popcorn, popped (1/2 cup unpopped
   popcorn kernels)
1/2 cup honey-roasted peanuts

Directions:

1. Place one candy corn into each finger of the
   plastic glove.
2. Mix together popcorn and honey-roasted
   peanuts. Fill glove with mixture.
3. Stuff end of glove with raffia and tie closed
   with a single raffia strand. For decoration,
   place plastic toy ring on ring finger of hand.

Pumpkin People

Things You'll Need:
knife (parent only)
cutting board
small bowls
white glue
small hats
small play earrings
Ingredients:
various fall fruits and vegetables
small pumpkins
parsley (for hair)

Directions:

1. Before the activity, cut up several fall fruits and
   vegetables to use as facial features.
2. Place vegetables in small bowls.

3. Give each child a washed pumpkin. Ask them to glue the fall vegetables onto the pumpkin to create their own pumpkin faces.

4. Accessorize each pumpkin with hats, earrings, and parsley hair for a unique look. Be sure to mention that we, just like pumpkins, are all different on the outside, some small, some large. But we are the same on the inside, and all loved by God.

Easy Harvest Apple Dumplings

Things You'll Need:
apple corer
2 small bowls
pastry brush
9 x 13-inch pan
leaf cookie cutters
knife (parent only)
wax paper
Ingredients:
4 medium-sized apples
1 stick margarine
1/2 cup brown sugar
1 teaspoon cinnamon
1/4 cup raisins
2 prepared pie crusts
1 egg yolk

Directions:

1. Cut each pie crust in half and place dough on wax paper.

2. Wash and core apples. Dry and place each apple on a square piece of pie crust.

3. Stuff apples with brown sugar, cinnamon, margarine, and raisins.

4. Brush the outside of pastry with egg yolk, and bring the edges of the pie dough to the top of the apple.

5. Using a cookie cutter, cut leaf shapes out of leftover pie dough and stick to the egg yolk–brushed apple dumpling.

6. Bake dumplings according to pie crust package directions.

The Pretty Pumpkin

Things You'll Need:
bundt pan
large bowl
medium bowl
spoons
wax paper
electric mixer
measuring cups
measuring spoons
large plate
Ingredients:
2 white cake mixes
2 tablespoons pumpkin pie spice
3 cans prepared white icing
1 ice cream sugar cone
orange food coloring
green food coloring

candy corns
raisins

Directions:

1. Prepare one cake in the bundt pan according to package directions, adding half the pumpkin pie spice.
2. Remove cake from the bundt pan and prepare the other, adding the second half of the pumpkin pie spice. Cool thoroughly.
3. On a large plate, place one cake flat side up. Place the other cake on top of the first cake, right side up.
4. Place 2 1/2 cans of the icing in one bowl and mix in orange food coloring; stir to combine. Add the green food coloring to the remaining 1/2 can of icing. Ice the cake with the orange icing.
5. Ice the sugar cone with the green icing. Place the cone upside down in the center of the top cake for the pumpkin stem.
6. Using candy corn and raisins, create a face for the "pumpkin."

ART ADVENTURES

Pumpkin Patch Packages

Things You'll Need:
1/2 yard of orange material
tape

fabric paint pens
brown paper lunch bag
rubber band
child safety scissors
white glue
rubber band
green raffia
green construction paper
wax paper or pieces of
    newspaper
popcorn, candy corn,
    honey-roasted
    peanuts

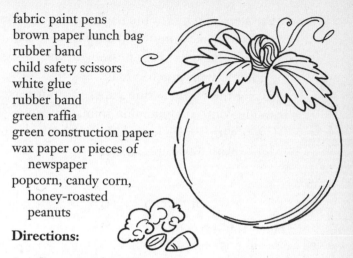

Directions:

1. Cover work surface with wax paper or news-paper, taping it to work surface to keep it secure.

2. Place brown paper bag in the center of the unfolded orange material and fill the bag with popcorn, candy corn, and honey-roasted peanuts.

3. Place crumpled newspaper around the paper bag. (This will help form the shape of the pumpkin once the orange fabric is pulled up and around the bag.)

4. Gather all the ends of the orange material to the top of the paper bag, wrapping a rubber band around the top of the material and the top of the paper bag to form the stem. Push

the stem down into the bag to round out the bag and make a pumpkin shape.

5. Secure the stem once more with the rubber band; tie with green raffia.

6. Using the construction paper, cut out leaves to glue onto the pumpkin stem. Give away as a gift with a note letting the person know to look inside for a special treat.

Corncob Prints

Things You'll Need:
corncobs, with corn on them
tray with sides
red, yellow, and orange tempera paint
paint smocks
paper towels
3 aluminum pie plates
white butcher paper

Directions:

1. Wash and thoroughly dry corncobs.

2. Prepare paint pads by folding paper towels and placing several in each pie plate. Pour paints onto the paper towels.

3. Line a sided tray with white butcher paper.

4. Roll the corncob on the paint pad, then place it on the paper-covered tray and roll it around for a unique fall design.

Fresh Fall Wreath

Things You'll Need:
colorful fall leaves
heavy paper plate
scissors (parent only)
white glue
raffia

Directions:

1. Go for a walk to collect as many soft fall-colored leaves as you can find.
2. Cut out the center of the paper plate, leaving a 3-inch band around the outside of the plate.
3. Glue different leaves around the outside of the plate, completely covering the white of the plate.
4. Allow leaves to dry completely.
5. Loop raffia through center of the plate and tie at top for a handy hanger.

Bean Leaf Mosaic

Things You'll Need:
heavy construction paper
white glue
tray with sides
variety of dried beans
leaf-shaped cookie cutter

Directions:

1. Pour several different colors of dried beans onto a tray.
2. Place the cookie cutter on the construction paper and draw an outline of the cutter with glue. Remove cutter.
3. Fill in the entire leaf shape with a thin layer of glue.
4. Glue all different types of beans over the glued surface.

Pumpkin Pop

Things You'll Need:
clear plastic soda pop bottle with twist-off cap
tablespoon
orange tempera paint
paint smocks
black felt
green felt
craft glue
scissors (parent only)

Directions:

1. Empty and rinse plastic soda bottle. Remove label. Allow to dry.
2. Pour 2 tablespoons orange paint into the bottle. Place cap back on bottle.

3. Swirl the orange paint all around inside the bottle so that the entire inside of the bottle looks orange.

4. Cut out eyes, nose, and mouth from black felt. Glue onto the bottle for a face.

5. Cut a green piece of felt large enough to cover the entire bottle cap and glue it to the bottle cap to resemble pumpkin leaves.

Fish Hugging

As a mother comforts her child, I will
comfort you.

Isaiah 66:13

READ...

Inspiration & Fun From MOPS just for Ages 2-4

Mommy, May I Hug the Fishes?

Written by Crystal Bowman
Illustrated by Donna Christensen

By: Crystal Bowman
Published by: Zondervan

HUGGING FISHES AND GIVING them kisses? In this book the imagination of a little preschooler requires a parent's guiding hand to help him set limits and say no to circumstances that could cause harm. Questions from the youngster as he goes through his day put Mom in the role of both answer woman and safety officer.

TEACHING TIPS

When your toddler gets mad or frustrated, she may throw herself down on the floor and kick and scream. Or perhaps she cries or throws a toy or a book. Self-control—the ability to control your own actions—is something most young preschoolers have very little of. You as the parent must say yes and no numerous times in order to direct your child.

Use this time to talk with your child about not interrupting when you are having a conversation with someone else. Together, make up signals you can give her to acknowledge that you know she is still waiting on you, and that you will speak with her as soon as you are through. Let her know that this is an important way she can show respect and self-control.

God wants us to live abundantly, but under his direction. Just as mothers want the best for their children, our heavenly Father wants the best for us.

RECIPES

Chocolate Cake Cookie Sandwiches

Things You'll Need:
cookie sheet
cooking spray
large bowl
spatula
electric mixer
measuring cups
tablespoon
cooling rack
plastic wrap
wax paper
fish stickers

Ingredients:
1 (18.5-ounce) package chocolate cake mix
your favorite flavor of ice cream

Directions:

1. Preheat oven to 350 degrees.
2. Spray cookie sheet with cooking spray.
3. Prepare cake mix as directed on the package, but reduce water by 1/2 cup.
4. Drop dough by rounded tablespoonfuls three inches apart onto the prepared cookie sheet.
5. Bake 8 to 10 minutes or until almost no impression remains when cookie is touched lightly.

6. While cookies are baking, apply fish stickers to the wax paper.
7. Remove cookies and place on cooling rack. After cookies have cooled, turn them upside down and place a spoonful of ice cream between two cookies. Wrap cake cookies in plastic wrap first; then in the fish-covered wax paper. Place in freezer until ready to eat. Makes 1 dozen.

Fish Hugs

Things You'll Need:
plastic bag
new small bait pails
Ingredients:
2 cups fish crackers
1 cup gummy worms
1 cup pretzel-flavored fish crackers
1/2 cup miniature M&Ms
1/2 cup minimarshmallows

Directions:

1. Place all ingredients in a plastic bag and shake.
2. Pour into small bait pails and serve to your favorite fish-hugger.

Teddy Pops

Things You'll Need:
cookie sheet

rolling pin
thick skewers or lollipop sticks
teddy bear-shaped cookie cutter
Ingredients:
1 package prepared sugar cookie dough
variety of tube frostings
cinnamon red hot candies
decorative sprinkles

Directions:
1. On a lightly floured surface, roll out the cookie dough to about a 1/2-inch thickness.
2. Spray cookie sheet with cooking spray.
3. Cut the dough with a teddy bear cookie cutter and place cookies on the cookie sheet.
4. Gently insert skewers right into the middle of the cut cookie thickness. Push the skewer all the way up to the top of the cookie.
5. Bake according to package directions. Cool and frost. Add red hot candies for eyes and sprinkles for clothes.

Praying Hands Snacker Crackers

Things You'll Need:
sifter
plastic knife or fork
measuring spoons
2 cookie sheets
2 mixing bowls
whisk
rolling pin

pastry brush
Ingredients:
cooking spray
1/2 teaspoon dry mustard
1/2 cup mild cheddar cheese, grated
1 cup all-purpose flour
1/4 cup margarine, chilled
1 egg

Directions:

1. Preheat oven to 350 degrees.
2. Spray cookie sheets with cooking spray.
3. Sift flour and dry mustard together in a mixing bowl.
4. Cut margarine into flour using a plastic knife or the back side of a fork, until dough looks like marbles or peas. Mix in cheese.
5. Break the egg into another mixing bowl and beat with a whisk. Add 2 tablespoons of whisked egg to flour mixture and stir to combine.
6. Knead dough on a floured surface. Roll to about 1/2-inch thickness. Place two little hands on the rolled-out dough and cut around them with a plastic knife.
7. Place dough hands on the cookie sheet; lightly brush with remaining egg mixture. Bake for 12 to 15 minutes.
8. When cooled, place hands together to form praying hands. Try placing a slice of lunch meat in between for a "hand" sandwich.

Storybook Sandwiches

Things You'll Need:
cutting board
table knife
plate
2 squirt bottles
Ingredients:
2 slices white bread
2 tablespoons peanut butter
1 tablespoon jelly
1 package red string licorice

Directions:

1. Place each piece of bread on a cutting board and cut off crusts, making a square out of the bread pieces; place the two pieces of bread side by side on a plate.

2. Where the bread slices meet, make two sets of holes in each piece of bread directly across from each other.

3. For the storybook "binding," cut the red string licorice into 1 1/2 inch pieces and thread from one hole of one bread slice to the hole on the other bread slice.

4. Place peanut butter in one squirt bottle and jelly in the other. On one piece of bread scribble lines of peanut butter to resemble words on a page. On the second piece of bread, scribble lines of jelly, or draw a picture with the jelly to resemble the inside of a storybook.

ART ADVENTURES

Fish Frames

Things You'll Need:
plain plastic frame
white glue
several small plastic fish

Directions:

1. Place the plastic frame on a clean work surface.
2. Glue plastic fish around the perimeter of the frame. Dry thoroughly.
3. Ask a parent or friend to take a picture of you and your mom reading *Mommy, May I Hug the Fishes?* and put that picture in the fish frame.

Yes and No Signs

Things You'll Need:
shirt cardboard or poster board
child safety scissors
stapler
markers
alphabet stickers
long popsicle stick

Directions:

1. Cut two 6-inch circles from shirt cardboard or poster board.
2. Place two circles together. Put the long popsicle stick in the center of the circles and staple around the entire outside area.
3. Select the correct letters from alphabet stickers to spell "yes." Place the stickers on one side of the sign.
4. Select the correct letters from alphabet stickers to spell "no." Stick those letters to the other side of the sign.
5. Decorate yes and no signs with markers.

My Two Feet

Things You'll Need:
butcher paper
markers

Directions:

1. Roll out a long piece of butcher paper for the street. Place both feet on the butcher paper and trace around feet with a marker.
2. Take a step, then trace feet again. Continue this process until you have used up your entire piece of butcher paper.

A Fish to Kiss

Things You'll Need:
coat hanger
aluminum foil
crayons
decorative wiggly eyes
white glue

Directions:

1. Press coat hanger into the shape of a diamond.
2. Tear off two sheets of aluminum foil and color completely with several colors of crayon.
3. Tear aluminum foil into strips and wrap them around the entire diamond-shaped coat hanger.
4. Glue a wiggly eye on the aluminum where the fish's face would be.

The Real Reason for the candy cane season

God loved the world so much that he gave his
one and only son.

John 3:16

READ ...

By: Lori Walburg
Published by: Zondervan

ON A VERY COLD and dark November night, a strange man rides into a small prairie town. All of the townspeople are very curious to know who he is, why he is in town, and what he is doing. Everyone hopes he will be someone who can help them; even the children hold deep secret wishes. One day a little girl named Lucy offers to help the man, and in helping him she learns a wonderful lesson. Lucy then shares the lesson or "legend" of the candy cane with everyone in her town.

TEACHING TIPS

Transform your neighborhood into candy cane lane with the following fun activity. Prepare peppermint play dough with your child (see recipe section). As you form the candy canes with the play dough, discuss the true meaning of Christmas and the legend of the candy cane.

Place two or three real candy canes and some peppermint play dough in a decorated Christmas sack. Include the story of the candy cane written out on decorative Christmas paper. Give as gifts to your friends and neighbors.

RECIPES

Peppermint Play Dough

Things You'll Need:
medium saucepan
wooden spoon
medium bowl
wax paper

Ingredients:
1 cup all-purpose flour
1/2 cup salt
2 teaspoons cream of tartar
1 tablespoon cooking oil
1 cup water
several drops red food coloring
4 drops peppermint oil
2 tablespoons glitter

Directions:

1. In a medium saucepan, mix dry ingredients. Add oil and water and stir over heat until combined.
2. Take off the stove. Divide mixture in half. Add red food coloring to one batch and leave the other plain.
3. Cook the plain batch first, stirring constantly over low heat until mixture forms a ball in pan. Remove from pan.
4. Repeat process for red batch.
5. Knead each batch separately, adding two drops of peppermint oil and 1/2 tablespoon of glitter into each.

6. Place the two batches of play dough on wax paper and divide each into four or five pieces. Roll into long strands. Twist one red and one white strand together to form a candy cane. Pinch ends together and bend into candy-cane shape. Sprinkle candy canes with remaining glitter and let dry.

Peppermint Fudge

Things You'll Need:
medium saucepan
wooden spoon
cooking spray
9 x 9 glass baking dish
Ingredients:
1 1/2 cups sugar
2/3 cup evaporated milk
1/2 teaspoon salt
2 cups minimarshmallows
1 1/2 cups semi-sweet chocolate chips
10 peppermint candies, crushed
1/2 teaspoon peppermint extract
1 teaspoon vanilla extract

Directions:

1. In a medium saucepan, mix sugar, milk, and salt over low heat.
2. Bring to a boil and simmer for four minutes.
3. Remove from heat and add marshmallows, chocolate chips, crushed peppermint candies, and extracts. Mix well.

4. Spray glass dish with cooking spray. Pour mixture into dish and refrigerate until firm. Cut into 1-inch squares to serve.

Flower Gumdrops

Things You'll Need:
toothpicks
plastic wrap
ribbon
Ingredients:
assorted gumdrops

Directions:

1. Stick five toothpicks into the top of five gumdrops.
2. Stick the other end of the five toothpicks around the entire perimeter of one large gumdrop, to create a flower.
3. Cover with colored plastic wrap, tie closed with a ribbon.

Peppermint Christmas Cream

Things You'll Need:
large bowl
electric mixer
spatula
measuring cups
measuring spoons

resealable plastic bag
rolling pin
Ingredients:
1 cup heavy cream
1 cup powdered sugar
2 teaspoons vanilla extract
1 quart (4 cups) clean snow
6 to 8 small candy canes

Directions:

1. Place candy canes in plastic bag and seal. Roll over the plastic bag with a rolling pin until candy is crushed. Set aside.
2. Whip the cream until soft peaks form; fold in the sugar and vanilla.
3. Fold fresh, clean snow into the cream mixture.
4. Top with crushed candy canes and eat immediately, or put the well-covered bowl outside your door in a snow bank and let it chill until ice cream has hardened.

Butterscotch Mangers

Things You'll Need:
small bowl
spoon
paper plates
Ingredients:
1 (15-ounce) container chow mein noodles
1 (8-ounce) jar of marshmallow cream
1 (6-ounce) bag butterscotch chips

Directions:

1. Pour chow mein noodles into a bowl.
2. Stir in half of the marshmallow cream.
3. Sprinkle half the bag of butterscotch chips into the mixture; stir to combine.
4. Spoon two tablespoonfuls of the mixture onto a paper plate and form into a manger. A yummy treat! Makes 10 mangers.

ART ADVENTURES

Candy Cane Ornaments

Things You'll Need:
2 cups flour
1 cup salt
1 cup cold water
large spoon
large bowl
white acrylic paint
red paste food coloring (found in most cake decorating stores)
wax paper

Directions:

1. Preheat oven to 325 degrees.
2. Stir together flour, salt, and water.
3. Knead mixture until it forms a stiff dough. To add color, take small portions of the dough and work in little dabs of red paste food coloring.

Color the white portion with white acrylic paint.

4. Roll equal size pieces of each color into ropes and twist together. Cut the twisted strip to desired length and bend to form a curved top. Bake ornaments for 1 to 1 1/2 hours, or until dried.

Candy Cane Lane

Things You'll Need:
miniature candy canes in long cellophane
    wrappers
ribbon
little bells
scissors (parent only)
red yarn
green yarn

Directions:

1. Cut ribbon into 6-inch strips. Thread a small bell onto each ribbon.
2. Tie the ribbons in between each wrapped candy cane. Hang finished row of candy canes on the wall by your front door.
3. Wrap the handles of a pair of scissors with red and green yarn.
4. As guests leave your home, cut off a bow and bell-tied candy cane as a parting gift.

Peppermint Stick Container

Things You'll Need:
empty soup can or glass jar
hot glue gun (adults only)
candy canes, unwrapped
peppermint fudge or paperwhite flowers
   (optional)

Directions:

1. Using a hot glue gun, attach unwrapped candy canes to the outside of an empty soup can or glass jar. Continue to glue candy canes side by side until the entire container is full.
2. Tie a ribbon around the middle of the jar. Fill with peppermint fudge or use for planting paperwhites (white flowers used at Christmas).

Lollipop Lane

Things You'll Need:
10-inch round, 1-inch thick disk of Styrofoam
   (available at craft stores)
colored cellophane or plastic wrap
long dowel about 1 inch in circumference
colorful wide ribbon
twist tie

Directions:

1. Insert dowel into the bottom of the Styrofoam disk.

2. Wrap a large piece of colored cellophane or plastic wrap over the Styrofoam disk.
3. Using a twist tie, fasten the cellophane where the dowel and disk meet.
4. Cover the twist tie with a ribbon. A perfect decoration for doors or walls. Or make a bunch and line your sidewalks with lollipops.

Starry, Starry Night

Things You'll Need:
dark blue construction paper
brown construction paper
nativity scene picture, from coloring book
straw
white glue
animal stickers
large star sticker
small metallic star stickers

Directions:

1. A few weeks before Christmas, place the nativity picture from the coloring book on top of a piece of brown construction paper. Trace the outline of the stable and cut it out. Then glue the brown construction paper stable onto dark blue construction paper.
2. Glue some straw around the bottom of the stable.

3. Place animal stickers inside and outside the stable.

4. Every time the child does something good (following directions, being nice to siblings, avoiding a fight with classmate, etc.), he or she gets to place another star in the sky above the stable. By Christmas, you should have a beautiful, starry night sky to welcome baby Jesus!

AfterWord

SNUGGLING INTO YOUR FAVORITE comfortable spot and opening a brightly illustrated, creatively written book offers the ultimate in relaxation. When you teach your child to relax this way, you are not only nurturing them, you are teaching them to nurture themselves.

Imaginative activities can greatly enhance the joy that togetherness brings. I encourage you to take your child's favorite stories and use them to adapt your own cooking and art activities. Know your child's likes and dislikes and tailor your ideas to fit the bill. Then watch as their enthusiasm and zest for learning begins and their imagination soars!

I wish you the very best as you become all God created you to be as a mom.

About This Busy Mom

AFTER GRADUATING FROM BAYLOR University, Jane began her career with *Southern Living* magazine, where she organized and directed cooking shows all over the South. She has written seven books and coauthored five books and fourteen curriculum titles. She has appeared on numerous television and radio talk shows. Jane and her husband, Mark, have one daughter, Sarah, and live in Texas.

MOTHERS OF
M♥PS®
PRESCHOOLERS

MOPS stands for Mothers of Preschoolers, a program designed to encourage mothers with children under school age through relationships and resources. These women come from different backgrounds and lifestyles, yet have similar needs and a shared desire to be the best mothers they can be!

A MOPS group provides a caring, accepting atmosphere for today's mother of preschoolers. Here she has an opportunity to share concerns, explore areas of creativity, and hear instruction that equips her for the responsibilities of family and community. The MOPS group also includes MOPPETS, a loving, learning experience for children.

Approximately 2,500 groups meet in churches throughout the United States, Canada, and 13 other countries, to meet the needs of more than 100,000 women. Many more mothers are encouraged by MOPS resources, including *MOMSense* radio and magazine, MOPS' web site, and publications such as this book.

Find out how MOPS International can help you
become part of the MOPS©to©Mom Connection.

MOPS International
P.O. Box 102200
Denver, CO 80250-2200
Phone 1-800-929-1287 or 303-733-5353
E-mail: Info@MOPS.org
Web site: http://www.MOPS.org

To learn how to start a MOPS group,
call 1-888-910-MOPS.
For MOPS products call The MOPShop
1-888-545-4040.